Regulations for Small Vessels

A Guide to Operating Vessels Commercially

by **Simon Jinks**

© RYA
First Published 2012
Reprinted June 2013
Reprinted August 2015
The Royal Yachting Association
RYA House, Ensign Way, Hamble,
Southampton, SO31 4YA
Tel: 0844 556 9555
Fax: 0844 556 9516
Email: publications@rya.org.uk
Web: www.rya.org.uk
Follow us on Twitter @RYAPublications
or on YouTube
ISBN: 978-1-906435714
RYA Order Code: G105

A CIP record of this book is available from the British Library

Note: While all reasonable care has been taken in the preparation
of this book, the publisher takes no responsibility for the use of
the methods or products or contracts described in this book.

Cover design: Design House
Photographic credits: Simon Jinks, Stuart Jenkins, Turbine
Transfer, QHM Plymouth, Williams Shipping, IMO, Maritime and
Coastguard Agency. LOF and its supporting documents have been
reproduced with the kind permission of Lloyd's.
Typeset: Creativebyte
Proofreading and indexing: Alan Thatcher
Printed in China through World Print Ltd.

Totally Chlorine
Free

Sustainable
Forests

FOREWORD

There are more than 20,000 people working commercially in the marine industry on RYA commercially endorsed qualifications and certificates of competence. The vast majority of those people have progressed through from recreational boaters into the commercial marine environment.

While the practical skills and competencies required for recreational boaters are very similar to those needed in the commercial world there are some significant differences that set boating purely for pleasure apart from boating in a commercial environment.

This book is designed to give those using RYA qualifications on a commercial basis a good understanding of their obligations as Master of a commercial vessel of less than 200gt. The book is specifically written to support the "RYA Professional Practices and Responsibilities" course that underpins all RYA commercial qualifications but is also a useful reference for operators working commercially on small vessels anywhere in the world.

Ignorance of the law or of local regulations is no defence and the maritime environment is one of the more complex regulatory frameworks in which to work. I hope this book assists you in better understanding your obligations as a professional Master, and enables you to make decisions on the management and safety of your vessel, crew and passengers with greater confidence.

Richard Falk
RYA Training Manager & Chief Examiner

CONTENTS

INTRODUCTION

Whether you are a Skipper, owner, operator or crew, there are responsibilities when you venture afloat and these increase when the boat operates commercially. The principles of commercial operation are very similar the world over, as many maritime laws and regulations have their origins in international conventions. By and large, when working commercially around the world, there's often a common theme of safety and how you manage it.

While there is much written about what equipment to carry, there is precious little about what systems to adopt to ensure the boat runs safely and efficiently. This book gives guidance on what is required for safe operation and identifies your responsibilities to the boat, those around you and the environment.

The book covers all craft operating commercially from commercial RIBs and day sailers up to 200gt (gross tonnage) vessels. The 200gt ceiling reflects the initial limit of the RYA Yachtmaster Ocean and Offshore Certificates of Competence. This qualification allows the holder to skipper pleasure and commercial vessels up to 200gt. Other RYA skippering qualifications mentioned in this book are limited to 24 metres. The RYA Yachtmaster Offshore qualification is then the start of a career pathway for skippering vessels up to 3000gt. Above 3000gt, the qualification structure is defined with the STCW (Standards of Training, Certification and Watchkeeping) convention.

While large commercial vessels are catered for in international law, smaller vessels, pleasure boats and those under 80gt or 24m are often exempted. In practice, this means each individual country decides how much of a law applies depending on how smaller craft are used. This often allows a pragmatic view so that small craft are not lumbered with unnecessary and inappropriate equipment or legislation.

PART 1:
THE LEGAL FRAMEWORK

Sources of Law (International and Domestic)

The Rule Makers

There are those organisations who make the rules, those bodies and authorities who adopt and implement them, and the rest of us (owners, operators, Skippers and crew), who abide and work within them.

Maritime legislators and regulators are split into international, continent-specific, national and local bodies. Often an international law is adopted and it is applicable to all vessels over a certain tonnage; under a certain tonnage (usually small vessels) it can be interpreted in slightly different ways when applied throughout a continental area or nationally by a government. Let's start with the top maritime rule maker.

UN/IMO

The International Maritime Organization (IMO) is a specialised body of the United Nations responsible for improving the safety and security of international shipping and preventing marine pollution. The IMO's membership is made up of about 170 states (countries).

To improve safety and security and prevent pollution, the IMO produces conventions, which are detailed rules that have been discussed and debated by all the IMO member states. The conventions are adopted by a government and the country's shipping policy changes to reflect the convention. Finally, it enters into the maritime law of the country. There are well over twenty conventions but the main five are arguably:

- UNCLOS
- International Convention for the Safety of Life at Sea (SOLAS)
- International Convention for the Prevention of Pollution from Ships (MARPOL)
- International Convention on Standards of Training, Certification and Watchkeeping for Seafarers (STCW)
- Convention on the International Regulations for Preventing Collisions at Sea (IRPCS)

International regulations usually come from the United Nations.

The United Nations developed UNCLOS (United Nations Convention on the Law of the Sea), which provides a framework for the use of the oceans. This convention specifies the territorial limits of a country and defines whether a vessel is under the laws of the country in which it is registered or the country in which it is lying. UNCLOS identifies the roles of flag, coastal and port state, what a country has to do to identify and register its ships and how it controls ships entering its coastal/territorial waters and ports. UN also has regional commissions in Asia, Latin America, Africa and Europe dealing with transport and shipping in those areas.

Two lesser known but relevant conventions are on load lines and tonnage. Both cover how a boat is measured and registered within a country. Importantly, they suggest that vessels less than 80gt or 24m, fishing vessels and pleasure vessels can be exempted from measurement and registration. On this historical basis many subsequent conventions use these exemption references and, as such, pleasure vessels and vessels under 80gt are often exempted from the full international regulation allowing a nation to decide what is best applied.

1998 No. 2241

The Merchant Shipping (Load Line) Regulations 1998

PART I

GENERAL

Application

4.—(1) These Regulations apply to United Kingdom ships wherever they may be and to other ships while they are within United Kingdom waters, except—

(a) ships of war;

(b) ships solely engaged in fishing;

(c) pleasure vessels;

(d) ships which do not go to sea; and

(e) ships under 80 tons register falling within one of the classes specified in paragrah (2) engaged solely in the coasting trade, and, subject to paragraph (3), not carrying cargo—

(2) Those classes are—

(a) tugs or salvage ships;

(b) hopper barges or dredgers;

(c) ships used by or on behalf of—

   (i) a general or local lighthouse authority for the purpose of the authority's functions as such;

   (ii) a Government department for fishery protection purposes, or a local fisheries committee for the regulation of sea fisheries within its district;

   (iii) a Government department for fishery or scientific research; or

   (iv) the Secretary of State for Defence for the purpose of ensuring safety in the use of firing ranges or weapons at sea; and

(d) ships in respect of which passenger certificates are in force specifying limits beyond which the ship must not ply, and which operate solely within those limits;

(e) ships carrying not more than 12 passengers for sport or pleasure on a voyage in the course of which they are at no time more than 3 miles from land nor more than 15 miles from their point of departure, unless the point of departure lies within Category A, B, C or D waters, when the distance of 15 miles shall be measured from the seaward boundary of such limits.

(3) A ship referred to in paragraph (1)(e) falling within the class in paragraph (2)(d) shall be excepted from the provisions of these Regulations while carrying cargo in accordance with the terms, if any, of the ship's passenger certificate expressly authorising the carriage of cargo.

For instance, the Collision Regulations (COLREGs) apply to all vessels but the requirements for lights, shapes and sound signals change depending on vessel size. The training and manning requirements in STCW are exempted for most pleasure craft but can be applicable to small commercial vessels. SOLAS mainly covers larger vessels however Chapter V is applied to pleasure craft and smaller vessels. The UN/IMO also produce guidelines, which are not binding.

UN/UNECE

The United Nations Economic Commission for Europe (UNECE) is one of the five regional commissions of the UN that aims to bring together co-operation and standards within the 56 European countries and North America. Probably the most well-known resolutions UNECE worked on are Resolutions 14 and 40. They created the International Certificate for Operators of Pleasure Craft (ICC) as a means of facilitating its holders voyaging internationally to countries that have signed up to accept the certificate.

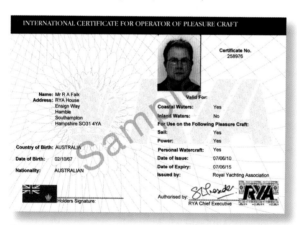

An ICC certificate.

EU

The European Union is made up of 27 member states and produces directives and regulations that affect Europe such as the use of passports within EU countries, and the Recreational Craft Directive concerning the standards of build of vessels between 2.5m and 24m. It is currently working on a harmonisation process to establish an Integrated Maritime Policy (IMP) for the European Union. It is envisaged that the IMP will enhance the way maritime affairs are managed in Europe.

Small Craft Regulation

All small craft encounter some type of regulation and law. The regulations applied almost globally are the COLREGs, SOLAS V, UNCLOS and MARPOL. It is best to consider these laws as always applying whatever the country you are in and the flag you are under. If the vessel is run commercially then a whole host of other regulations and guidelines creep in. The level of legislation often depends on the geographic location, the vessel size and regulatory arrangements within the country.

SOLAS

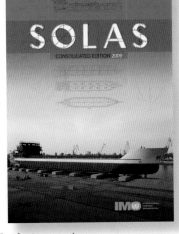

The Safety of Life at Sea Convention (SOLAS) includes 12 chapters covering lifesaving appliances, fire protection, radio communications, security and safe operation of ships but it is Chapter 5 – Safety of Navigation – that has the most far-reaching regulation for small craft. While most of the convention applies to large commercial vessels this section is aimed at all vessels, including small commercial and pleasure craft. The key requirements are:

- **Safe navigation**

    This requires the Skipper to consider and plan the passage taking into account several seamanlike factors such as weather, tidal streams, limitations of the boat and the crew, checking charts for navigational dangers and having a contingency plan for longer voyages. The plan does not necessarily need to be written down but it would be difficult to prove that you complied if it were not. The detail of the plan depends on the complexity and length of passage.

- **Radar reflectors**

    The regulation requires carriage and preferably permanent mounting of a radar reflector. If your boat is more than 15m in length, you should be able to fit a radar reflector that meets the IMO requirements of 10m^2 radar cross section (RCS). If your boat is less than 15m in length, you should fit the largest radar reflector you can. In the UK the Maritime & Coastguard Agency (MCA) recommends permanently mounting a radar reflector with the highest RCS.

- **Assistance to other craft**

    You are required to help anyone in distress as best you can and report anything you encounter that could cause a serious hazard to navigation to the Coastguard or authorities.

- **Lifesaving signals**

    A set of internationally recognised signals has been adopted for communicating between ships, aircraft and persons in distress. An illustrated copy of these should be kept on-board. They are often included in the almanac or pilotage notes.

- **Misuse of distress signals**

    You undertake not to misuse or falsely send distress messages.

These regulations are not enforced on a day-to-day basis but may be when there is an incident. Insurers may look closely at your actions with respect to SOLAS V in the event of a claim.

COLREGs

The International Regulations for Preventing Collisions at Sea (IRPCS or COLREGs) apply to all vessels upon the high seas and connected waters navigable by seagoing vessels.

It is essential that you know these rules so you are aware when you are the stand-on vessel, when you are the give-way vessel and understand the correct action to take to avoid a collision.

The level of signalling equipment and lights carried changes with the vessel's length and usage. Rules concerning the carriage and use of lights, sounds and shapes change as size increases. There are other parts of COLREGs that vary depending on the length of the vessel.

STCW

The International Convention on Standards of Training, Certification and Watchkeeping is an attempt to standardise seafarers' basic training requirements around the world. The first convention was in 1978 and was amended significantly in 1995. The latest convention was held in Manila in 2010. The STCW convention covers the training requirements for the Master, deck, engine, radio communication and safety and survival personnel on-board.

Pleasure vessels are exempted from the STCW convention, but the MCA implements some of the training requirements for commercial Skippers and crews working overseas on UK vessels or vessels of another flag. UK-flagged vessels over 24m increasingly require manning with STCW-compliant certification.

Possibly the most relevant section of STCW for vessels under 200gt is the guidance given in Chapter VIII on how to structure voyage planning and watchkeeping. (Annex 1).

MARPOL

MARPOL (MARine POLlution) is the International Convention for the Prevention of Pollution from Ships. The convention aims to minimise pollution from all boats, whether it is accidental pollution or from routine operations. There are six annexes, each identifying a particular type of pollution.

- Annex 1 Prevention of pollution by oil
- Annex 2 Control of pollution by liquid noxious substances in bulk
- Annex 3 Prevention of pollution by harmful substances carried by sea in packaged form
- Annex 4 Prevention of sewage from ships
- Annex 5 Prevention of pollution by garbage from ships
- Annex 6 Prevention of air pollution from ships

Annexes 1, 4 and 5 are of most interest to the smaller vessel as they concern diesel spillages, black and brown water discharges and the management of garbage. The implications of MARPOL change around the world depending on the geographical area as some countries have a heightened sensitivity regarding pollution and increase legislation accordingly. For instance, in tidal waters holding tanks are rarely required, whereas Mediterranean and Scandinavian countries stipulate more stringent use and pump-out procedures.

The effects of MARPOL on UK-flagged small vessels:

- The discharge of oil from the bilge or bilges should not exceed 15 parts per million (leaving an oily smear on the water).

- Vessels over 12m should display placards notifying passengers and crew of garbage disposal arrangements.

- Vessels carrying more than 15 persons require a garbage management plan and a higher tech sewage system or holding tank.

- Penalties for contravention of MARPOL can be severe and have been some of the largest ever given.

MLC

In 2006 the International Labour Organisation (ILO) published the Maritime and Labour Convention (MLC), and this came into force in 2013. The convention covers many seafarer standards. The MLC does not apply to vessels navigating exclusively within inland or sheltered waters or to ships operating on domestic voyages within 60 miles of a UK safe haven. A domestic voyage is a voyage that starts and finishes in the UK without the vessel going to a port in another state. Therefore a code vessel travelling on an international voyage will need to be MLC-compliant and require additional inspection. This is achieved by the certifying authority inspecting the vessel and its documentation. A successful MLC survey will result in the SCV certificate being endorsed as complying with the UK implementation of the MLC. This could be used voluntarily for operators to gain the Maritime Labour Certificate from the MCA. Certification and survey last for a maximum of 36 months. Probably the greatest changes affecting smaller vessels are the requirements for Seafarer Employment Agreements (crew contracts) with employees who work afloat and the auditable compliance with the Hours of Work and rest regulations.

Maritime and Flag State Authorities

The flag state of a vessel is the state under whose laws the vessel is registered (UNCLOS Articles 91 and 94). The flag state has the responsibility to enforce regulations, including those relating to inspection, certification, and issuance of official documentation. The authority of the flag state is usually transferred to the maritime authority for the country.

UNCLOS also states how far to sea the country has control. There are many different areas but, for our purposes, possibly the most important are coastal and port state. A country with a coastline is empowered to manage its coastal state, often defined as its territorial sea, which is approximately up to 12 miles offshore. While a country cannot prevent innocent passage, it can adopt laws on the safety of navigation, prevention of pollution and protecting its seabed. It can also insist that vessels transiting within the coastal state comply with international law and convention (UNCLOS Articles 19 and 21).

Port State Control (PSC) is the inspection of foreign ships, large or small, in national ports to verify that the condition of the ship and its equipment complies with international rules and regulations. Merchant vessels tend to be the main targets, especially ships requiring a higher degree of safety such as oil and chemical tankers and passenger ships.

English Law

English law has formed the template law for many flag states. The classes of English law most relevant to seafarers are common law, criminal & statute law, civil and Admiralty law.

Common law is the so-called 'unwritten law' based on accepted norms and customs, judgments and judicial precedent. Judicial precedent is the precedent set by a previous case which then may develop a principle in law that is adopted or referred to in similar subsequent cases.

Statute law is an Act of Parliament, order, rule or regulation made under statute and is the primary source of English law. Closely linked to statute law is criminal law, which deals with breaking laws against the state; the state is therefore the prosecutor. Laws laid down by the state in the marine world are statutes such as the Merchant Shipping Act and secondary regulations like the Merchant Shipping Regulations. Penalties are fines and imprisonment, referenced to a pre-defined scale of penalties.

Civil law is concerned with the rights and responsibilities of people and companies towards each other. There are no punitive sanctions such as imprisonment, but damages may be awarded by the judge from one party to the other. Cases covered in civil law are often to do with breach of contract, property, negligence or Admiralty law.

It is possible that a person can be prosecuted under criminal law by the state and then have a civil action taken against them by an injured party because they have also been negligent.

Admiralty law covers those parts of the law that are strictly to do with seamanship and navigation such as collisions, salvage and damage. Admiralty law is handled in a civil court.

Merchant Shipping Legislation

UK Regulation

In the UK, Merchant Shipping Regulations normally apply to all vessels under the UK flag and to vessels in UK waters or operating from UK ports.

An SI (Statutory Instrument) contains the majority of UK law. Statutory Instruments are created on the orders of government ministers who have that power granted by Parliament by an Act.

Exemptions to the regulations are granted within the legislation. The size of a vessel, the number of passengers it carries and whether or not the vessel is used solely for pleasure are factors determining which regulations apply. Pleasure vessels are often exempted from many of the regulations whereas commercial vessels need to comply with the Merchant Shipping Regulations.

It is important to determine what regulation applies and the starting point is establishing how you and your boat are defined within the rules.

Definitions

- **'Categorised waters'** – Waters that are not classed as sea
- **'Class XII vessels'** – Pleasure vessels of 13.7m in registered length and over
- **'Large yacht'** – A vessel over 24m load line length
- **'Owner/managing agent'** – The owner, or managing agent of the owner of the vessel
- **'Passenger'** – Any person not employed or engaged in the business of the vessel
- **'Passenger ship'** – A vessel that carries more than 12 passengers regardless of its size
- **'Pleasure vessels'** – Used for sport or pleasure by the owner or his family and friends – but not for commercial gain
- **'Small vessel'** – A vessel of less than 24 metres in load line length
- **'To sea'** – Proceeding outside categorised waters

Pleasure Vessel

There is no definition of a commercial vessel other than one that is not a pleasure vessel; therefore we need to establish whether the vessel is a pleasure vessel or not.

The broad definition of a 'pleasure vessel' is any vessel which, at the time it is being used, is:

(i)   used only for the sport or pleasure of the owner or the immediate family or friends of the owner; or if owned by a corporate body, used only for sport or pleasure and the persons on-board are employees or officers of the body corporate, or their immediate family or friends; and

(ii) on a voyage or excursion which is one for which the owner does not receive money for or in connection with operating the vessel or carrying any person, other than as a contribution to the direct expenses of the operation of the vessel incurred during the voyage or excursion, and no other payments are made by or on behalf of users of the vessel, other than by the owner; or

(iii) a vessel owned by a members' club formed for the purpose of sport or pleasure and used only for the sport or pleasure of members of that club and for the use of which any charges levied are paid into club funds and applied for the general use of the club; and no other payments are made by or on behalf of users of the vessel, other than by the owner.

If the boat you operate is not a pleasure vessel it is deemed to be working commercially. At this point merchant shipping regulations applicable to commercial vessels apply.

If it is a pleasure vessel an equipment regulation comes in at 13.7m when the boat is deemed a Class XII vessel.

Class XII Vessels

Boats over 13.7m/45ft registered length are classified as being in Class XII as defined by the Merchant Shipping Regulations. They are obliged to carry certain fire-fighting and lifesaving appliances. The exact type and quantity varies depending upon how far the boat cruises offshore but the equipment list includes liferafts, lifebuoys, lifejackets, flares, instruction manuals, marine radio, fire extinguishers and fire buckets.

COSWP

The Code of Safe Working Practices (COSWP) is primarily intended for seamen on UK-registered vessels. It is a helpful guide to managing the safety of employees and a copy of COSWP must be carried on all UK ships other than fishing vessels and pleasure vessels. COSWP is really based around large ships; however, its principles can be translated to small vessels. If you employ people to work on board a boat, including the self-employed, you should ensure the operating and safety practices you adopt are in the spirit of those within COSWP.

COSWP gives guidance on:
- Carrying out risk assessments
- Identifying early signs of ill health caused by occupational hazards
- Developing a safety culture on-board
- Providing personal protective equipment
- Signage for health and safety information
- Maintenance of plant, machinery and equipment
- Safety induction training to all new workers
- Taking measures to prevent fires on-board including fire and emergency training
- Maintain high levels of on-board security to avoid illegal activities
- Promoting personal health and hygiene standards among staff and the preparation and storage of food

Accident Reporting Responsibility

Many countries and flag states have an official maritime accident or incident reporting system. They do so to satisfy international resolutions from the IMO and European Parliament directives and, as such, create a national policy for the investigation into the accidents and incidents.

The IMO ... *requests flag States to conduct an investigation into all very serious and serious marine casualties...*
(IMO resolution A.849 (20))

The underlying principles are that:

... investigations into marine casualties improve maritime safety, as it helps to prevent the recurrence of such casualties resulting in loss of life, loss of ships and pollution of the marine environment. (Directive 2009/18/EC Of The European Parliament)

The norm is that you report the accident 'as soon as practicable' and quite often this can be done online, by fax, phone or using an accident report form. If you are unsure who to contact in the event of a serious accident, contact your maritime authority.

MAIB

In the UK accidents are reported to the Marine Accident Investigation Branch (MAIB) or the Health and Safety Executive (HSE). The MAIB investigates accidents relating to ships and crew. The HSE investigates land-based and offshore installation accidents and there are times of obvious overlap when the MAIB and HSE work together. If you are unsure, so long as you report to one organisation, you will be advised accordingly and the report passed to the other.

For instance, the HSE would be interested in the loading of passengers and stores to and from the vessel, or the vessel while ashore, whereas the MAIB area of concern would grow as the boat unties its lines. More often than not, it will be the MAIB that you would first contact and be advised accordingly.

Department for Transport and Agencies

National

Governments accept or interpret conventions and regulations to establish their own merchant shipping regulations and empower marine authorities to legislate and regulate those laws. This allows a certain amount of pragmatism when dealing with leisure and small commercial craft so that it is suitable. The levels of exposure, risk and concerns over pollution may be different if you are in Germany, Greece or on a loch in Scotland, so a marine authority may heighten or lessen the regulation to suit.

Regulators
Maritime and Flag State Authority

In the UK the MCA is the flag state and port state control. As a ship operates under the laws of its flag state, these laws are used if the ship is involved in prosecution under maritime law for offences committed on the High Seas and can also consider prosecution under both British and domestic law when in foreign waters.

Radio Licensing

Stray radio waves could cause havoc if they were not regulated and the thought of emissions from a boat's microwave oven affecting those of the radar are best not considered. They are considered by the International Telecommunications Union (ITU), which regulates the airwaves. Ofcom is the UK administration to the ITU and deals with the licensing of radio equipment and its use. The Ship Radio Licence allows the licensee to install and, if the relevant Maritime Radio Operators' Certificate of Competence and Authority to Operate is held, use any combination of maritime radio equipment listed below on a specified vessel.

- Digital Selective Calling (DSC) equipment associated with the Global Maritime Distress & Safety System (GMDSS):
- MF, HF, VHF equipment
- Satellite communications equipment (Ship Earth Stations)
- RADAR
- Search and Rescue Radar Transponders (SARTs)
- Low-powered, on-board maritime UHF communications equipment and UHF repeater stations
- 121.5/243MHz and 406/121.5MHz Emergency Position Indicating Radio Beacons (EPIRBs)
- 1.6 GHz EPIRBs
- Personal Locator Beacons (PLBs)

Local Authorities and Harbours

Local Authorities have the ability to regulate and enforce local regulations in their jurisdiction. While they generally accept national standards, occasionally they may set their own when waters are inland, or within harbour limits. Regulations can govern the equipment that the vessel carries and the way that it is checked or licensed. Harbour authorities often publish their speed limits and important regulations in almanacs, pilot books, on the internet and through harbour authority publications.

Here is an example of a local harbour authority regulation from the Crouch Harbour Guide:

The River Speed limits apply to all Power Driven Vessels (except emergency services vehicles). The speed limit is 8 knots (8 Nautical Miles per hour = 9.216 land miles per hour) through/over the water. The limits apply at all times. Fine for breach: up to £1,000.

Regulatory Publications

A maritime authority publishes regulations, laws and good practice for the mariner. In the UK there are Statutory Instruments (see p.14) and M Notices.

Marine (M) Notices publicise important safety announcements, pollution prevention, and other relevant information. There are three types:

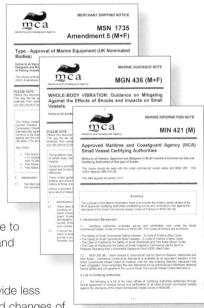

- Merchant Shipping Notices (MSNs) often contain the fine detail of the law and are legally enforceable when referred to in a Statutory Instrument.

- Marine Guidance Notes (MGNs) give guidance and strong recommendations about best practice to the industry on interpretation of law and general safety advice.

- Marine Information Notes (MINs) provide less important time-limited information and changes of address after which they expire.

19

If you are working commercially it is your responsibility to stay up to date on best practice and the law. Many flag states use an e-mail register to send out Notices as and when they become available.

Governing Bodies and Associations

Occasionally a governing body of a sport or association is given the authority via the government or maritime authority to administer a particular sector or type of craft. For instance, in the UK the RYA, SeaFish, British Sub Aqua Club and British Water Ski & Wakeboard have authority to issue licences and organise training for small craft. As providers of maritime training under the MCA, they are also audited by them.

PART 2:
REGULATION OF VESSELS

Ship Registration

Registration

In the maritime world registration is important as it links the vessel with the rules, regulations and also the rights of its flag state. In the UK, registration is optional for all vessels in UK waters. However, vessels under 24m are 'stateless' if they leave UK territorial waters unregistered, and in practice smaller craft may encounter difficulties with foreign administrations if they are not registered.

The Register of British Ships is divided into four parts:

- Part 1 is the traditional registration system tracing its routes back to the 16th century. It is available for all general shipping and small craft and is the only option if there is a mortgage secured to the boat, or if the boat is over 24m or company owned. Part 1 secures the title of the boat to the owner but is more involved to achieve as a new boat requires a tonnage measurement and existing boats require proof of ownership going back five years.

- Part 2 is for fishing vessels.

- Part 3 is the Small Ships Register (SSR) and is the cheapest and simplest way of registering a boat to sail to another country. In effect it is the yacht's passport.

- Part 4 was introduced to allow chartered-in foreign-owned ships to be British registered during the time of their charter, thus complying with the regulations of the UK flag.

British pleasure vessels can register under Part 1 or Part 3 so long as they fulfil the relevant ownership categories.

Be aware that if the boat is registered under another country's flag it will operate under the rules of that country's flag. That country may stipulate a type of skippering qualification that is only taught in their language and unless you have it or have agreed a dispensation you could be breaking the rules. If you skipper a boat under a different flag, ensure you are aware of any national and local laws.

Commercial Vessels

A vessel is working commercially if it is not a pleasure vessel. It then requires equipping and manning to standards laid down in the Merchant Shipping Regulations. Commercial small craft, even those over 24m, find it difficult to comply with large-ship requirements, so they are offered a different route whereby they can choose to comply with a specific Code of Practice which will exempt them from the Merchant Shipping Regulations. The actual Code of Practice that applies depends on the size and intended area of operation and the flag under which the vessel is registered.

Areas of Operation

The further the vessel operates from a safe haven, the more risk it is exposed to. It makes sense, therefore, that the construction standards, safety equipment and manning requirements increase with range and risk. Vessels are primarily licensed or coded for working within specific 'categorised waters' or 'at sea'.

Categorised Waters

In the UK, categorised waters are those deemed to be not 'sea' and offer a large degree of shelter and small wave height. These areas are canals, lakes, lochs, sheltered bays on the coast and estuaries. They are defined into four categories:

- Category A: Narrow rivers and canals where the depth of water is generally less than 1.5 metres.
- Category B: Wider rivers and canals where the depth of water is generally 1.5 metres or more and where the significant wave height could not be expected to exceed 0.6 metres at any time.
- Category C: Tidal rivers and estuaries and large, deep lakes and lochs where the significant wave height could not be expected to exceed 1.2 metres at any time.
- Category D: Tidal rivers and estuaries where the significant wave height could not be expected to exceed 2 metres at any time.

Region and Location	Category A, B or C	Category D
Plymouth	Category C within a line from Mount Batten Pier to Raveness Point through Drake's Island. The River Yealm within a line from Warren Point to Misery Point.	Within a line from Cawsand to Breakwater to Staddon.
Fowey	Category C inside the Harbour.	None
Falmouth	Category C within a line from St Anthony Head to Pendennis Point.	In winter within a line from St Anthony Head to Rosemullion Point. In summer within a line from St Anthony Head to Nare Point.

(Information taken from MCA Categorisation of Waters document)

The categories usually apply throughout the year but occasionally an area will change its category or expand during the summer months. 'Summer' means the months of April to October (inclusive) and 'winter' means the months of November to March (inclusive).

Vessels operating in categorised waters are often regulated by a local licensing system administered by the port or Local Authority. The MCA publishes an Inland Waterways Small Boat Passenger Code for vessels carrying fewer than 12 passengers. The code is a best practice guide for use by operators, designers, builders and competent authorities. It can be made mandatory by local competent authorities for use in their area.

To Sea

'To sea' is any area beyond Category D waters or Category C if there are no Category D waters. The regulations which then apply in the UK depend on whether the vessel is under or over 24m.

SMALL VESSELS are defined as vessels up to 24 metres 'load line length'.

LARGE VESSELS are those of 24 metres 'load line length' and over.

The MCA produces a Code of Practice for small and large commercial vessels. The codes contain safety requirements for the vessels and crew of commercially operated vessels carrying no more than 12 passengers, and are an acceptable alternative to the Merchant Shipping Regulations which would otherwise apply.

Small Vessels less than 24m

If the boat is under 24m and carries fewer than 12 passengers it will need to comply with one of the following codes:

- The Safety of Small Commercial Motor Vessels – A Code of Practice (Yellow Code)
- The Safety of Small Commercial Sailing Vessels – A Code of Practice (Blue Code)
- The Code of Practice for the Safety of Small Workboats & Pilot Boats (Brown Code)
- The Code of Practice for the Safety of Small Vessels in Commercial Use for Sport or Pleasure
- Operating from a Nominated Departure Point (NDP) (Red Code)

The codes are very similar and the overarching safety principles and requirements are the same – there are just differences on how they are applied to different types of vessels.

In 2004, the MCA published a harmonisation of the Yellow, Blue, Brown and Red codes under an M Notice titled Small Vessels in Commercial Use for Sport or Pleasure, Workboats and Pilot Boats. It is referred to as 'the harmonised code' or MGN 280.

The four 'coloured' codes have legal effect by virtue of a Statutory Instrument. However, the harmonised code has yet to be made law (2011). The M Notice that issued the harmonised code stated that it can be used to survey and code vessels as an equivalent standard. So, since November 2004, vessels could be assessed under the harmonised code or the individual codes.

The codes detail the construction standards, vessel equipment, certification and survey, qualifications, manning levels and the requirement of a system to manage the safety of the vessel.

The RYA is one of a number of organisations approved by the MCA as a Small Commercial Vessel (SCV) certifying authority to administer the examination and periodic inspection of small boats in commercial use. Others include:

- Bureau Veritas
- Burness Corlett – Three Quays Ltd
- International Institute of Marine Surveying
- Lloyd's Register
- MECAL Ltd
- RINA UK Ltd
- The Society on Consulting Marine Engineers and Ship Surveyors
- Yacht Designers and Surveyors Association
- Department of Transport
- Det Norske Veritas
- Seafish Marine Services

Sea Areas for Vessels under 24m

If the boat is less than 24m the various UK Codes of Practice for Small Commercial Vessels split the 'sea' up into seven area categories. The area category that the vessel is allowed to work in is decided by the certifying authority after establishing its stability. Vessel information is supplied to the certifying authority, calculations are made and the owner issued with a certificate defining the area category the boat can be coded up to.

> A vessel may be considered for the issue of a Small Commercial Vessel certificate allowing it to operate in one of the following areas:
>
> - Area Category 6 – To sea, within 3 miles from a nominated departure point(s) named in the certificate and never more than 3 miles from land, in favourable weather and daylight.
>
> - Area Category 5 – To sea, within 20 miles from a nominated departure point named in the certificate in favourable weather and daylight.
>
> - Area Category 4 – Up to 20 miles from a safe haven, in favourable weather and in daylight.
>
> - Area Category 3 – Up to 20 miles from a safe haven.
>
> - Area Category 2 – Up to 60 miles from a safe haven.
>
> - Area Category 1 – Up to 150 miles from a safe haven.
>
> - Area Category 0 – Unrestricted service.
>
> (Extract taken from MGN 280)

The equipment carried, qualifications of the Skipper and crew and required manning levels increase as the vessel goes further from land.

Large Vessels

Commercial vessels over 24m and less than 3000gt require coding to the Large Yacht Code (LY2). The code applies to vessels in commercial use for sport or pleasure which are 24 metres in 'load line' length and over but which do not carry cargo, or more than 12 passengers.

The code sets standards of safety and pollution prevention appropriate to the size and operation of the vessel. Standards are normally set by the relevant international conventions but the code provides equivalent standards as permitted by the conventions where it is not reasonable or practical to comply with the original convention.

A newer version of the Large Yacht Code (LY3) is being discussed and is presently (2012) in draft form.

There is an upper limit of 3000gt for deck officer qualifications specifically designed for yachts and sail training vessels. The general view within the industry was that any yacht of more than 3000gt should not be built to the Large Yacht Code but in accordance with the relevant IMO conventions.

Large Vessel Areas

Generally the regulations in LY2 allow worldwide unlimited operation. However a 'Short Range Yacht' category is included for vessels that cannot, or have no operational need to, meet the 'unlimited' criteria. This is particularly relevant to high-powered yachts with large engines that may not meet the stringent damage survivability requirements in relation to engine-room flooding.

The parameters for Short Range Yachts are:

- Less than 300gt (for new vessels) or Less than 500gt (for existing vessels).
- Operation up to 60 miles from a safe haven (this may be increased to 90 miles on specified routes with the agreement of the administration).
- Operation within favourable weather – Force 4 by forecast/actual.

Survey & Certification

Vessel Examination and Certification

Requirements for Small Vessels (under 24m) to be Examined and Certificated

The owner/managing agent of a vessel to be operated under the code, should:

- Choose an authorised certifying authority and contact them to obtain a copy of the appropriate application form for examination/survey.

- Complete the form and return it to the certifying authority with fees (when requested).

- Establish, with the certifying authority, the vessel's permitted area of operation.

- Arrange with the certifying authority for the vessel to be examined by an authorised person and documented in the appropriate report form for a Compliance Examination.

- Be in receipt of a valid certificate for the vessel prior to it entering into service.

- Regularly inspect the vessel and arrange survey and updated documentation to ensure compliance.

Requirements for Large Vessels (over 24m) to be Examined and Certificated

- The MCA Code is now established as the worldwide standard for Large Yachts. The MCA has a Large Yacht Unit (Ensign) that carries out the survey of UK commercial vessels over 24m.

- Ensign would carry out the plan approval and survey.

- The vessel's class society will be responsible for a large part of survey, comprising the hull and machinery.

- An Ensign surveyor would probably visit a minimum of three times, once at an early stage, once to witness stability tests (when construction is 98% complete) and a final visit on completion.

Vessel Certification

Following successful survey, certificates are issued to the owner. Often a certifying authority also issues a code disk that can be displayed in the window of the boat. Copies of the certification and code paperwork detailing the equipment carried should be carried on-board.

Code compliance certificates for both the small and large vessel codes are valid for five years.

Annual, intermediate and renewal surveys are required to keep the vessel compliant. By and large, annual surveys often check the vessel against its paperwork; intermediate surveys are physical checks on the equipment and condition of the vessel, and renewals are a full inspection including out-of-water inspection.

A typical MCA Small Commercial Vessel Certificate.

Operational Standards

Going to Sea

When a commercial vessel puts to sea it not only needs to have the correct equipment onboard and correctly qualified people manning it, it also needs to operate safely and to a set of standards.

Charter Operator

If the vessel is being bareboat chartered or hired out the owner/ managing agent is required to give a formal handover to the charterer. It covers how the vessel and its equipment operates, plus the contents of the paperwork file and vessel documentation. Details are contained in Annex 4.

Safety Brief

The Skipper of a vessel should ensure that each person on-board is briefed on safety in accordance with the requirements given in Annex 3.

Your vessel or the nature of your work may require more items to be covered in the brief. A note in the logbook or other suitable document should be made to verify the brief has been carried out.

Passage Planning

Planning your passage is a good idea anyway but the regulations laid down in SOLAS V (Regulation 34 – Safe navigation and avoidance of dangerous situations) make it a requirement:

The voyage plan shall identify a route which: takes into account any relevant ships' routeing systems; ensures sufficient sea room for the safe passage of the ship throughout the voyage; anticipates all known navigational hazards and adverse weather conditions; and takes into account the marine environmental protection measures that apply, and avoids, as far as possible, actions and activities which could cause damage to the environment.

The IMO's guidelines to voyage planning take on four stages:

- Appraising all relevant information
- Planning the intended voyage
- Executing the plan taking account of prevailing conditions
- Continuously monitoring the vessel's progress against the plan

Realistically this means that you will:

- Check the weather forecast and get regular updates
- Check the tidal and stream predictions
- Consider the limitations of the vessel and those implied by certification
- Consider limitations imposed by safety equipment, stores and fuel
- Take into account the experience and strength of the crew
- Ensure you are familiar with any navigational dangers by consulting and carrying up-to-date charts and publications
- Establish a contingency plan and bolt holes where safe refuge can be sought
- Ensure someone ashore knows your plans

The IMO provides guidance on voyage planning which has been adopted by many countries. For more information see 'IMO Guidelines for Voyage Planning, Resolution A.893 (21)' and 'International Convention on Standards of Training, Certification and Watchkeeping for Seafarers Chapter VIII'.

When operating locally and in an area of which you have in-depth knowledge, noting the day's changeable parameters such as streams, weather, vessel and crew may be sufficient.

Charts

All vessels which go to sea are required to ensure that the intended voyage has been planned using appropriate nautical charts and nautical publications… (Regulation 34 of SOLAS Chapter V)

Carrying relevant navigation systems and equipment (including charts) applies to all ships irrespective of size. Charts and publications should be up to date and there should be a system to keep them so. A chart plotter with electronic leisure charts is often not allowed as a stand-alone navigational tool but can be used alongside updated paper charts.

Publications

Nautical publications such as sailing directions, lists of lights, notices to mariners, tide tables and all other nautical publications necessary for the intended voyage shall be adequate and up to date. Small craft Almanacs are sometimes allowed instead of carrying individual copies of radio signals, stream atlases etc. (Regulation 27 of SOLAS Chapter V)

When travelling to another country a copy of that country's regulations is often required.

Use of Logbooks

The Merchant Shipping (Official Log Book) Regulations 1981 make it a requirement for all United Kingdom commercial vessels (except ships less than 25gt and pleasure vessels) to carry and keep an official logbook.

Vessels under 25gt are well advised to carry and complete a logbook as it is a record of the passage and events. It will be the first document required by the authorities in the event of an incident.

Vessel Traffic Services

As vessel size increases or when it changes from pleasure to commercial, so do its reporting responsibilities to a Vessel Traffic Service (VTS) such as port operations or harbour control. Vessel Traffic Services monitor the traffic within a specified area and they will record what size/type of vessel reports when they pass a certain point. Often a radio reporting symbol is placed on the chart; the direction of the arrow indicates whether reporting is required for inbound or outbound traffic or both.

Local Notices/Regulations

Nearly every harbour has its own set of local regulations. These are often local speed limits, limits of anchorage and your environmental duties but, occasionally they also concern the rights of way of vessels. This could be giving a right of way to a chain ferry, greater rights of vessels travelling with the stream or changing the rights of vessels dependant on size and direction.

An example of a Local Notice to Mariners taken from the Queen's Harbour Master Plymouth website.

Part 3: The Skipper & Crew

Training & Certification

Manning and Certification

Manning requirements are the prescribed amount and level of crew involved in running the boat. They are prescribed by a code of practice and by common sense. For instance, Rule 5 of the IRPCS calls for 'a proper lookout by sight and hearing as well as by all available means..'. Therefore a boat will need to be manned to ensure there is always an adequate watch. A code of practice may require a 23m vessel to have just a second person to help run the boat; however, a 23m sail-training ship may require more staff to ensure the boat runs efficiently and safely.

It is the owner or managing agent's responsibility to ensure the boat is safely manned.

When a boat operates commercially it has to come up to a certain specification and so do the Skipper and crew. The level of qualification required by the Skipper is often dictated by the distance the boat travels offshore and the number of people it carries. For instance, in the UK a vessel less than 24m operating up to three miles from a nominated departure point requires a Day Skipper qualification whereas a boat operating up to 60 miles from a safe haven requires an RYA Yachtmaster Offshore qualification.

Additionally, extra crew members should be on-board to ensure the safe operation of the vessel. If the boat does not venture too far offshore, the additional person could be someone who 'knows the boat' and is capable of assisting the Skipper in the event of an emergency.

Single-handed Operation

Commercial codes often do not like single-handed operation but accept it sometimes happens. Codes provide recommendations for persons working single-handed based on how far offshore the vessel operates, the duration, forecast and what extra safety equipment is required, such as the compulsory use of a lifejacket and the fitting and use of kill cords in open boats.

The immediate causes of the collision were the pilot failing to take avoiding action in sufficient time, and the fisherman failing to keep a proper lookout... Sailing single-handedly on fishing vessels is ill-advised... A minimum number of two crew on-board may have significantly reduced the risk of collision. (Extracts taken from the MAIB Safety Digest 2/2003 – Collision between an 8904gt Roll-on Roll-off ferry and a 14m fishing boat operating single-handed at night.)

Certification

A level of certification to prove competence is usually required if you are skippering or working on a commercial boat. The level of certification often changes depending on how far offshore the vessel is operating.

Additional Certification

The vessel also requires a person with a valid radio operator's certificate and a first aid certificate. These are pre-requisites for some qualifications and are usually required by all Skippers of a small vessel.

A vessel working under the Small Vessel Code of Practice requires the Skipper's certification to the levels in the table, plus additional crew.

Category 0	Unrestricted (i.e. worldwide)
Certificate required	RYA Yachtmaster Ocean Certificate of Competence
Category 1	**Up to 150 miles from a safe haven**
Certificate required	RYA Yachtmaster Offshore Certificate of Competence, or RYA Yachtmaster Ocean Certificate of Competence
Category 2	**Up to 60 miles from a safe haven**
Certificate required	RYA Yachtmaster Offshore Certificate of Competence, or RYA Yachtmaster Ocean Certificate of Competence
Category 3	**Up to 20 miles from a safe haven**
Certificate required	RYA Advanced Powerboat Certificate of Competence, or RYA Yachtmaster Coastal Certificate of Competence, or RYA Yachtmaster Offshore Certificate of Competence, or RYA Yachtmaster Ocean Certificate of Competence
Category 4	**Up to 20 miles from a safe haven, in favourable weather and daylight**
Certificate required	RYA Advanced Powerboat Certificate of Competence, or RYA Yachtmaster Coastal Certificate of Competence, or RYA Yachtmaster Offshore Certificate of Competence, or RYA Yachtmaster Ocean Certificate of Competence
Category 5	**To sea, within 20 miles from a nominated departure point (NDP) in favourable weather and daylight**
Certificate required	RYA Day Skipper Practical and Shorebased Certificate, or RYA Advanced Powerboat Certificate of Competence, or RYA Yachtmaster Coastal Certificate of Competence, or RYA Yachtmaster Offshore Certificate of Competence, or RYA Yachtmaster Ocean Certificate of Competence
Category 6	**To sea, within 3 miles from a nominated departure point(s) (NDP) and never more than 3 miles from land, in favourable weather and daylight**
Certificate required	RYA Powerboat Level 2, or RYA Day Skipper Practical Certificate, or RYA Advanced Powerboat Certificate of Competence, or RYA Yachtmaster Coastal Certificate of Competence, or RYA Yachtmaster Offshore Certificate of Competence, or RYA Yachtmaster Ocean Certificate of Competence

Commercial Endorsement

The small vessel codes of practice require personal certification of Skippers and often crew to be commercially endorsed. The RYA is the issuing body authorised by the MCA to administer these endorsements. A commercial endorsement requires a medical fitness certificate and an RYA or STCW Sea Survival Course certificate. There are various types of medical certificates accepted, some of which only allow operation up to 60 miles from a safe haven and it is up to the holder to ensure they hold the correct one for the passage.

On receipt of the medical and sea survival certificates, the original Skipper's certificate is stamped with a commercial endorsement.

As of April 2012 candidates for commercial endorsement will also need to complete the RYA online Professional Practices and Responsibilities (PPR) course.

There are two types of commercial endorsement:

- For RYA Yachtmaster Offshore and RYA Yachtmaster Ocean Certificates of Competence: *This certificate is valid for use as a Master of yachts of up to 200gt in accordance with UK Merchant Shipping Regulations until (date of expiry)*

  Valid for commercial use on vessels subject to the codes of practice issued by the Maritime and Coastguard Agency until: (date of expiry)

- For Powerboat Level 2, Powerboat Advanced, Day Skipper and RYA Yachtmaster Coastal Certificates of Competence: *Valid for commercial use on vessels subject to the codes of practice issued by the Maritime and Coastguard Agency until: (date of expiry)*

Validity

The maximum time a commercial endorsement is valid for is five years. Occasionally, restrictions are applied to shorten the validity; they are usually due to expiry of the medical certificate or based on a medical condition. It is important to check certificates for 'restrictions'.

Skippering Non-UK-Flagged Vessels

A Skipper's certification usually needs to reflect the flag of the vessel. For instance, Spanish authorities may require a Spanish-flagged pleasure or commercial vessel to be skippered by someone with a Spanish licence. If you are skippering a Spanish pleasure vessel up to 60 miles you require the *Patron de Yate*; if you are skippering the same yacht commercially, you may additionally need the *Patron Professional de Embarcacion Recreo.*

Sometimes, if you are working on-board a non-UK-flagged boat, your RYA certificates might be acceptable but you will need to comply with the rules of the flag state. An additional STCW endorsement may help holders of the RYA Yachtmaster Offshore and Ocean Certificates of Competence working under non-UK maritime authorities. It requires four additional STCW courses:

- Personal Survival Techniques (STCW A-V1/1-1)
- Personal Safety and Social Responsibilities (STCW A-V1/1-4)
- Elementary First Aid (STCW A-V1/1-3)
- Fire Fighting and Fire Prevention (STCW A-V1/1-2)

The following wording would appear on your RYA Yachtmaster Offshore/Ocean certificate:

The holder of the certificate has been trained to the standard of STCW78 as amended, V1/1 Sections V1/1-4. This certificate is valid for use as a Master of yachts of up to 200gt on commercially and privately registered yachts until (date of expiry)

MCA Master (Yacht) and Officer of the Watch (Code vessel less than 200gt – 500gt–3000gt)

RYA qualifications are the entry point and stepping stone into MCA Master (Yacht) and Officer of the Watch (OOW) qualifications. These are useful on coded boats under 200gt when transiting overseas and are also a manning requirement on larger vessels up to 3000gt. They use STCW courses to form the basic training, and the level of required experience, sea time, training and subsequent examination increases with tonnage.

The Master (Code vessel less than 200gt) is very similar to the RYA Yachtmaster Offshore but can be useful when operating from foreign ports when the port officials are more used to recognising MCA or flag state

qualifications.
In some cases
overseas
administrations
allow seafarers
to operate other
flagged vessels
if they hold an
MCA certificate
referencing STCW.

The basic requirements for Master 200 are:

- RYA Yachtmaster Offshore or Ocean Certificate of Competence plus shorebased certificate

- Certificates for the four elements of STCW basic training:

    • Personal Survival Techniques (STCW A-VI/1-1) or non-STCW RYA Basic Sea Survival

    • Fire Fighting and Fire Prevention (STCW A-VI/1-2)

    • Elementary First Aid (STCW A-VI/1-3)

    • Personal Safety and Social Responsibilities (STCW A-VI/1-4)

- A GMDSS Restricted Operators Certificate (ROC) or General Operators Certificate (GOC)

- Pass the Master (Code vessels less than 200gt) oral examination with the MCA

The Master 200 comes in two levels; 'limited', allowing operation up to 150 miles from a safe haven, or 'unlimited' for worldwide use. Holders of RYA Yachtmaster Offshore with a ROC GMDSS certificate are limited to 150 miles. RYA Yachtmaster Ocean holders with a GOC GMDSS certificate are classed as unlimited.

The RYA Yachtmaster Offshore and Ocean Certificates with commercial endorsement are valid for use on UK flagged vessels up to 200gt, not carrying more than 12 persons. If you are running vessels over 200gt the qualifications required and manning levels are published in MCA MSN 1802.

RYA and MCA qualifications

RYA and MCA certification go hand-in-hand. Commercially endorsed certificates can be used professionally in their own right as a stepping-stone to other MCA qualifications and the RYA Yachtmaster Offshore.

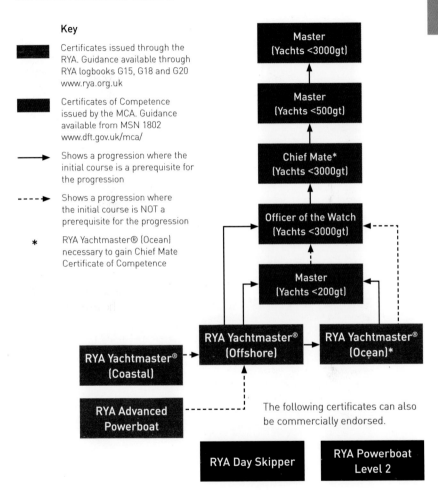

Key

Certificates issued through the RYA. Guidance available through RYA logbooks G15, G18 and G20 www.rya.org.uk

Certificates of Competence issued by the MCA. Guidance available from MSN 1802 www.dft.gov.uk/mca/

→ Shows a progression where the initial course is a prerequisite for the progression

- - -► Shows a progression where the initial course is NOT a prerequisite for the progression

* RYA Yachtmaster® (Ocean) necessary to gain Chief Mate Certificate of Competence

Master (Yachts <3000gt)

Master (Yachts <500gt)

Chief Mate* (Yachts <3000gt)

Officer of the Watch (Yachts <3000gt)

Master (Yachts <200gt)

RYA Yachtmaster® (Offshore)

RYA Yachtmaster® (Ocean)*

RYA Yachtmaster® (Coastal)

RYA Advanced Powerboat

The following certificates can also be commercially endorsed.

RYA Day Skipper

RYA Powerboat Level 2

Passengers and Trainees

Most Small Commercial Vessel (SCV) regulations concern vessels carrying less than 12 passengers. As soon as the tally goes above 12 passengers a whole load of regulation comes in classifying the boat as a passenger boat. Exceptions to this are those ferries operating within harbours or sheltered water, which are covered directly by the MCA under the Boat Master Licence and Scheme (BML). The scope of this book is limited to vessels carrying 12 passengers or fewer.

A passenger is loosely defined as any person who is not employed or engaged on the boat, allowing crew to be on-board also. Therefore a boat may have 12 passengers and four crew, making a total complement of 16 on-board.

Trainees

A trainee is loosely interpreted as someone who is on-board solely for the purpose of receiving instruction in responsibility, resourcefulness, loyalty and team endeavour; instruction in navigation and seamanship; to participate in the operation of the vessel and be part of the voyage crew but not form part of the safe manning complement. This may increase the number of people on-board considerably, but if the number is over 12 the authorities should be informed so that it can be established whether the operation is safe.

Health & Safety (Safe Working)

Responsibilities

When a vessel is operated commercially the owner, managing agent and Skipper have a legal responsibility to ensure that the boat is safe, properly manned and managed.

The law states: *'It shall be the duty of the owner (or operator) of a ship ... to take all reasonable steps to secure that the ship is operated in a safe manner'.* (Section 100 of the Merchant Shipping Act)

'...the Master or any seaman does any act, or is negligent in their duty, which causes or is likely to cause... the loss or serious damage to his or another ship, machinery, equipment or structure... or the death or serious injury to a person' (Section 58 of the Merchant Shipping Act)

Responsibilities are to passengers/trainees, the Skipper, crew and those employed or contracted to work on-board. The overall responsibilities include:

- *The health and safety of anyone working on-board; to be aware of any risks affecting workers and ensure that measures are taken to minimise them through improving procedures or equipment. To instruct those affected about the risks and how to ensure their own health and safety and the health and safety of others.* (MGN 20 or COSWP)

- *To ensure the vessel is properly maintained, examined and manned in accordance with the Code and in accordance with manufacturer's recommendations or best engineering practice.*

- *To ensure the Skipper and, where necessary, the crew have the required qualification and recent and relevant experience of the type and size of vessel, the machinery on the vessel, and the type of operation in which the vessel is engaged.*

- *To ensure there are sufficient additional crew on-board taking into account the type and duration of voyage/excursion being undertaken.*

- *The owner shall not prevent or restrict the Master of the ship from taking or executing any decision which, in the Master's professional judgement, is necessary for safe navigation and protection of the marine environment.*

Safe Manning and Hours of Work

Qualifications and Training

The Skipper and crew require relevant in-date qualifications. While qualifications are relatively generic, it is the operator's responsibility to ensure the boat is manned by people with the relevant experience on the type of boat and for the required work.

Crew should receive familiarisation training for on-board procedures. Even experienced crew may not be aware of a particular type of engine-starting system or the way a large winch is best handled. While they may have extensive experience, consider familiarising on the idiosyncrasies such as:

- Mooring and anchoring
- Launching and recovery of liferafts
- Evacuation from the vessel
- Donning of lifejackets
- Use and handling of fire-fighting equipment
- Use of lifting equipment or winches
- Vessel specifics, sails, towing, electronics

Lines of Communication

The responsibilities and authority of each employee or other crew member should be clear. This may be illustrated in a simple diagram showing who reports to whom. For instance, it could show the communication in an emergency situation or under what circumstances someone on watch refers to the Skipper. A simple list of events positioned near the chart table could clearly identify what warrants calling the Skipper on deck, such as:

Call the Skipper if:

1. An approaching vessel is on a collision course
2. You see lights or shapes that are not understood
3. There are changes in actual wind or sea conditions
4. Engine starting
5. Making a landfall
6. You are two hours prior to reaching port
7. Visibility reduces
8. There are accidents or near misses
9. You are unsure...

The requirement for reporting accidents should be well understood by all personnel and in so doing improve the safety culture practised on-board.

Procedures for Responding to Emergency Situations

The potential emergencies likely to be encountered on-board should be considered. There should be clearly stated procedures for responding to emergency situations such as:

- Fire
- Collision
- Grounding
- Engine or steering failure
- Man overboard
- Evacuation

Exercises and training should be carried out in the handling of emergencies and evacuation. Where possible, all personnel should be involved in these exercises, both ashore and afloat. The exercises and the names of those who participated should be recorded.

The roles and responsibilities of the crew in an emergency situation should be defined, so the Skipper, First Mate and Bosun know what they need to do or prepare.

Job Responsibilities

Writing down who is responsible for what job is a useful way to ensure that crew know their role. Those designated within the organisation as safety officer, engineer or first aider, their roles and what they do to fulfil them, should be noted. This helps them in remembering what they need to do and reminds the operator/Skipper if the role is not fulfilled.

The delegation of responsibility to a crew member for a specific role does not diminish the overall responsibility from the Skipper or owner.

Working Hours

There are many regulations concerning the hours of work and the treatment of seamen, such as the Maritime Labour Convention, EC Working Hours Directive and STCW.

Fatigue at sea is a serious safety issue and operators should ensure that all vessels certificated under the Code are sufficiently manned to avoid the need to work excessive hours. The Skipper is responsible for ensuring, so far as is reasonably practicable, that he/she and all crew members are properly rested when they begin work and obtain adequate rest when not on duty. The minimum hours of rest for anyone employed on-board should be not less than: Ten hours in any 24-hour period; and 77 hours in any seven day period. (Extract from MGN 280)

Skipper's Powers and Duties

Skipper's Authority and Responsibilities

The Master has authority at all times, to make decisions with regard to the safety of the vessel and the persons on-board. To ensure that there is no ambiguity regarding the authority of the Master, there should be a simple written statement.

The Master/Skipper of the boat has ultimate responsibility for the safe navigation of the ship and the prevention of marine pollution. The owner, the charterer, the company operating the ship, or any other person, cannot prevent or restrict the Skipper from taking or executing any decision which, in the Skipper's professional judgement, is necessary for safe navigation and protection of the marine environment.

The Skipper's responsibilities include:

- Implementing the safety policy on-board

- Ensuring the crew observe the policy

- Reporting all navigational hazards to the appropriate authority as soon as possible

- Completing the ship's log

- Ensuring that specified requirements are observed, i.e. manning, equipment, operating limits

- Ensuring that planned maintenance is carried out

- Carrying out safety briefings to passengers including the use and location of lifesaving equipment

- Training of crew in emergency procedures

- Pre-sailing vessel checks

- Ship's management and pilotage

- Vessel shut-down and security

- Mooring and berthing

Safe Management of the Vessel

The main requirement for the owner and the Skipper is safety. Therefore, a system to manage the safety of the vessel is a good place to start. The IMO requires vessels over 500gt to comply with the International Safety Management (ISM) Code and produce a Safety Management System. Both large and small vessel codes require a 'system to manage safety', therefore the requirements are similar. A brief explanation of the formal ISM Safety Management System (SMS) structure is in Annex 7.

The SMS, or your version of it, should reflect and support the operation. If you are a one-man operation with a small vessel, your system will be smaller than a company with a 24m vessel and 10 relief Skippers and 40 relief crew. Here are the key items in an SMS.

Owner's Responsibilities

The owner/managing agent is responsible for ensuring the boat is correctly equipped, manned and certified for the intended voyage. They should also develop a safety structure and operating procedures to which the vessel should be run. The Skipper carries out the owner's wishes and implements and sometimes advises on the procedures.

A useful reference for merchant seamen compiling a system is 'A Code of Safe Working Practices' (COSWP). COSWP is a helpful guide to managing the safety of employees afloat. A copy must be carried on all UK ships other than fishing vessels and pleasure craft. If you employ people on-board, including the self-employed, you must comply with the health, safety and working practice standards laid out within COSWP. Much of COSWP is for larger craft and it should be read with a healthy dose of common sense when applied to small vessels. However, the principles are the same. It covers:

- Carrying out risk assessments
- Identifying early signs of ill-health caused by occupational hazards
- Developing a safety culture on-board
- Providing personal protective equipment
- Signage for health and safety information
- Maintenance of plant, machinery and equipment
- Safety induction training to all new workers
- Taking measures to prevent fires on-board including fire and emergency training
- Maintaining high levels of on-board security to avoid illegal activities
- Promoting personal health and hygiene standards among staff
- Ensuring the correct preparation and storage of food

Risk Assessment

Carrying out a risk assessment will identify the different type and level of risk. If the assessment is expanded into how the boat should be run and maintained, it can also identify what procedures need to be in place for the safe operation and maintenance of the vessel.

The concept of risk assessment is relatively simple, and follows these basic steps:

- Identify the hazards and personnel at risk
- Assess the chances of a hazardous event occurring
- Assess the severity or consequences
- If the combined risk and severity is too great, some action should be taken to reduce the risk to as low a level as reasonably practical

A Health and Safety policy

This addresses the issues of health, safety and the environment as they affect the company and its staff. Such a policy might read along the following lines:

"The policy of [name of company/owner] is to conduct its activities taking full account of the health and safety of its employees and of all persons using or connected with the [company/owner]. In implementing this policy, [name of company/owner] will ensure that the [vessel] is, at all times, properly maintained and operated by qualified personnel in full compliance with relevant legislation. In particular the [company/owner] will carry out an assessment of the risks to the health and safety of workers and others affected by [the undertaking], and will take the necessary measures to minimise the risks identified." (Extract taken from LY2 Annex 2 (2))

It should include the following:

- One or more competent persons should be delegated to take responsibility for health and safety and their roles clearly defined.
- The lines of communication with the shore, in the event of an emergency.
- The policy for checking the vessel, equipment and certification.
- A policy on prevention of alcohol and drug abuse and the ramifications in law.

- A statement to the effect that it is still the responsibility of the owner/operator to ensure that the policy is complied with, and that the responsibilities are understood.
- A statement to the effect that while the owner/operator has the overriding responsibility; employees, passengers and trainees have a duty to take care of themselves and other persons who may be affected by their actions.

Operational Procedures

In short, the Health and Safety Policy is your declaration of intent to play by the rules and to take serious account of safety. It also states that the buck stops with you...

While the safety policy is the broad declaration it will need backing up with actual systems and procedures to ensure that the vessel complies with international, national and local regulations, maintenance, accident reporting and responding to emergencies – in short your operational procedures.

The procedures should be simple but ensure safe working practices are carried out. The procedures are *your* interpretation of how they will be carried out on *your vessel*. They may state how many people are on watch at a time, the policy for going aloft, checking the engine or disposing of garbage.

Often checklists can be used as prompt cards and signed off when completed. Checklists may be permanently exhibited such as in the wheelhouse for navigational items or laminated when used in an open vessel.

The major regulations to consider procedures for are:

- International Regulations for Preventing Collisions at Sea
- Local navigation rules
- National health and safety regulations
- The Code of Safe Working Practices for Merchant Seamen
- All relevant national shipping or guidance notices
- SOLAS V
- MARPOL

Annex 1 contains guidance on the composition of a navigational watch under STCW.

On-board and Maintenance Procedures

Simple procedures should be developed for the operation and maintenance of the vessel. These may include, but not be limited to:

- Sailing/sail hoisting and reefing procedures
- Testing of equipment, including steering gear, prior to commencing a passage
- Navigation and handling of the vessel
- Maintenance routines
- Refuelling and taking on water, gas etc.
- Watertight/weathertight integrity
- Stability of the vessel
- Conduct of passengers and crew while on-board

Maintenance and inspection may be split into a series of daily, weekly and monthly checklists. Time should be put aside for a more detailed inspection and maintenance programme of the vessel and equipment such as during a full or partial refit.

The frequency of the inspections should be determined by the owner/ operator, but every event should be recorded. A checklist could be employed as an aide memoire for the inspection.

Acceptance of a Safety Management System

Once the safety management system is written, it is important that all parties and employees read and understand it before it is put into place. In a new company, training may need to happen before the company officially starts to trade to ensure that requirements within the Safety Management System are met. A written statement by employees stating that they have read and understood the system is proof.

Good safety management is more about the organisation's culture than the paperwork. It is pointless having good written procedures if nobody follows them. For any system to work all involved must be actively engaged and understand their role in safety management. The written procedures are a communication tool and should simply assist all concerned in understanding their role and the role of others.

A good system will prevent any one person's mistake causing a major accident.

Review

Every company/owner should undertake a review of the Safety Management System at least once every three years. An external audit is a good back-up.

Record Keeping and Systems

Often the only way to prove that you have a system and that it works is by keeping a log or record of vital information. It also logs useful information such as when the last time the engine was serviced or that a certificate is about to expire. Record keeping should not be onerous but help you forward plan more effectively and record important facts.

Records should be kept and systems adopted for:

- Certification of vessel
- Certification and training of crew
- Expiration and service requirements for lifesaving equipment
- Maintenance of the vessel
- Safety checks carried out on-board the vessel
- Training and safety drills carried out

Certification of Vessel

UK-flagged commercial vessels are issued with a five-year licence requiring periodic, annual and mid-term inspection. Vessels should carry coding certification, insurance, a radio licence and, depending on the size and type of vessel, a garbage management plan, anti-fouling type disclosure etc. A record of the certificate and inspection expiry dates will help establish a plan for arranging inspections and refit. Refer to the relevant code under which you're operating.

Certification and Training of Crew

During busy times, it is easy for a certificate to be overlooked and fall out of date, but when it does the law is broken. This may mean that insurance policies also become invalid. The usual culprits are first aid, commercial endorsements and medical examinations which all have different times of validity.

*Certificate valid until *_____*maximum 5 years from date of issue or 65th birthday, whichever comes soonest. 1 year for those over 65 years of age (Extract from an ML5 medical certificate (MCGA)*

Vessel Maintenance

Can you imagine explaining to an investigator after an incident that you do maintain your vessel but, frustratingly, you are unable to prove it? Furthermore, do you sometimes forget the last time a part broke and you would really like to know so that you can establish a trend or consult the manufacturer? A maintenance record or defects book will help. There are parts of the boat that require regular maintenance; for instance on a daily, weekly, monthly and annual cycle. Listing those checks and simply noting that they have been completed forms a record.

On a day-to-day basis, if machinery fluid levels and engine temperatures/RPM are registered they can be monitored over time to see if there is a problem in the offing.

A booklet on-board containing breakages and repairs is a useful guide to an oncoming crew as to the current state of the vessel and its equipment.

Lifesaving Equipment (LSAs)

Almost all lifesaving appliances and fire systems have expiry dates. Occasionally a code will state that an item is to be serviced in line with the manufacturer's recommendation and therefore this needs to be established.

Safety Checks

Safety equipment will require checking to ensure that it is serviceable, has not been tampered with and is in a fit state ready for deployment.

Training and Safety Drills
There is often a legal requirement to give a safety brief to passengers before departure. Logging that this has been done ensures a record is kept in the event of an incident. For details of a safety brief see Annex 3.

The potential emergencies that could happen on-board should be considered and exercises undertaken with the crew to ensure they can deal with them. Record in the log when a drill was carried out and who was present.

Action before Expiry
Spreadsheets are often used to log expiry dates, but knowing that an item has expired today is of limited use. To ensure forward planning, establish a system that incorporates an action date so that a replacement can be obtained or an updating course arranged.

Accident Investigation and Reporting Systems

Reporting of Accidents

Vessels operating commercially may be required to report accidents to the maritime authority, so the company must have a procedure in place. Often forms are available via the authorities; if not, construct one so that you remember to take down the relevant information at the time. Accidents and near accidents should be recorded and reported to the operator/owner, who should implement corrective action with the aim of improving safety. In the UK, consult the Marine Accident Investigation Branch (p.17).

Initially, accidents should be reported to the Skipper and then back to the owner/managing agent. A vessel should have a system of recording and reviewing accidents and near misses to stop them happening again. While many accident books record the accident, the important part is what you do afterwards to stop its recurrence.

Accidents unfortunately do happen, but a recurring accident could be termed as negligence.

Accident, Incident and Near-miss Report Form

Date:	12/12/11	Time:	1307
Vessel:	The Beagle	Location:	Galapagos
Skipper & Crew:	Captain FitzRoy - C. Darwin		
Casualty/Vessels	C. Darwin		
Weather (wind, sea state, visibility, precipitation):			Calm

Time	What happened - who was involved - actions taken - lessons learned
1205	C. Darwin slipped on plastic hatch and fell onto his rear end. Bruised but no visible signs of pain or breakages.

Subsequent actions taken	
1215	Non-slip tape applied to all hatches and slippery surfaces and crew told to be vigilant for other such problems. Inspect tape during weekly safety checks.

What is an Accident?

The exact definition of an accident from the Merchant Shipping (Accident Reporting and Investigation) Regulations 2005 is in Annex 5, along with reporting requirements, and they can be summarised as follows:

- **Accident**

   An accident is an undesired event that results in personal injury, damage or loss. Accidents include loss of life or major injury to any person on-board, or when a person is lost from a vessel; the actual or presumed loss of a vessel, her abandonment or material damage to her; collision or grounding (unless deliberate or a brief touching with no damage caused), disablement, and also material damage caused by a vessel.

   A major injury includes any fracture to, or loss of, a limb, loss of sight, or any other injury requiring resuscitation or leading to hypothermia or admittance to a hospital or other medical facility for more than 24 hours.

   It is the duty of every Master or Skipper to examine any accident or major injury occurring to, or on-board, his/her vessel and report it to the MAIB. This reporting requirement does not extend to pleasure vessels.

- **Serious Injury**

   A serious injury is an injury, other than a major injury, when the injured person is incapacitated for more than three consecutive days. It should be reported within 14 days to the MAIB.

- **Hazardous Incident**

   A hazardous incident is when an accident nearly occurs in connection with the operation of a vessel. In other words, it is what is often known as a 'near miss'. The MAIB recommended that a report is submitted in the event of a near miss.

- **Publications**

   Accident investigation authorities provide publications which are useful to circulate around your staff and keep on-board. They provide a useful resource for lessons learned.

Criminal Liability (with Reference to the Merchant Shipping Act and Byelaws)

Law Enforcement – UK

Maritime authorities and governments enforce maritime rules by different methods. In general, maritime safety is directed through the maritime authority, in the UK it's the MCA. Realistically, the MCA compiles the evidence for the Crown Prosecution Service to act upon. There are also marine branches of the Police and Customs & Excise.

Jurisdiction

Sections 279 to 282 of the Merchant Shipping Act make it clear that the state has powers over UK-flagged vessels and seamen of any nationality working on them wherever the vessel may be. Therefore if an offence happens on a UK-flagged vessel in another country, the UK has jurisdiction to investigate and if required start legal proceedings.

Enforcement by Inspection

Certifying authorities regularly inspect vessels and if the vessel is not maintained to the standards required for compliance, the certifying authority can cancel the certificate.

The MCA has a significant inspection resource across the country comprising trained inspectors and a fleet of patrol boats capable of interception at sea and the boarding of suspect vessels. Checks are conducted on the currency of code vessel survey and certification records, on the appropriateness of certification for actual use and whether the boat is being operated within the Area Operation Category for which it is certified. Vessels can be served with an improvement notice or detained under the provisions of the Merchant Shipping Acts.

The usual problems are when a vessel operates:

- Beyond the category of operation
- Beyond the competence of the Skipper
- Under-manning
- Incorrect medical standards of Skipper and crew
- Incorrect or out-of-date medical kits
- Incorrect or improperly serviced GMDSS and lifesaving appliances
- Not complying with their own systems of operation

Public and passengers are increasingly aware of the type of regulation that a boat operates under, especially as the information is publicised online. Many an operator has been brought down by a hard done-by passenger calling the maritime authority with their concerns.

Inspection Overseas

Port State Control (PSC) is the inspection of foreign ships, large or small, in national ports to verify that the condition of the ship and its equipment complies with international rules and regulations. Large commercial vessels are the intended targets, especially ships that require a higher degree of safety such as gas carriers, oil and chemical tankers and passenger ships.

Factors that heighten a small commercial vessel's chance of being inspected by PSC are vessels which:

- *have been involved in a collision, grounding on their way to the port;*

- *have been accused of an alleged violation of pollution, or*

- *have manoeuvred in an erratic or unsafe manner or safe navigation practices and procedures have not been followed.*

(Extract taken from DIRECTIVE 2009/16/EC on Port State Control)

Enforcement by Prosecution

In circumstances where inspection identifies illegal operations, the MCA's enforcement branch will be notified. In the case of persistent and serious offenders, the enforcement branch takes the lead in preparing the casework for prosecution by the Crown Prosecution Service.

Courts hand down strict penalties for unsafe operations. Prosecutions are publicised on the MCA website. The MCA has records of all coded boats, large or small, so the public can check compliance.

The Law Courts

Legal proceedings are conducted through either a civil or criminal court.

Criminal courts deal with crimes against the state or the Crown such as breaches of statute or criminal law. The prosecutor is normally the 'state' and the defendant the 'accused' who has been summoned to court. This is expressed as, for instance, R v. Smith, 'R' being the abbreviation for Regina – the Queen or head of state – and Smith being the accused.

The type of criminal court the trial is held in depends on the severity of offence. Minor offences are tried in a Magistrates' Court and more serious offences in a Crown Court. Appeals are heard in a higher level court, such as a Court of Appeal or the House of Lords. In Scotland the criminal hearings will be held in a District Court, Sheriff Court, High Court of Justice or High Court of Justiciary in Edinburgh.

Civil courts deal with civil actions brought against one individual or company and another for non-'criminal' actions such as breach of contract, copyright infringement and the Law of Tort which encompasses a topic close to a Skipper or owner's heart – negligence. A hearing may be described as Smith v. Jones, Smith suing Jones for breach of copyright.

Civil actions are heard in civil courts ranging from a County Court to a High Court. The Admiralty Court is part of the High Court. Appeals are handled in the same way through either the Court of Appeal or House of Lords. In Scotland civil cases will be heard in the Sheriff Court, Outer House of the Court of Session or Inner House of the Court of Session.

When it goes Wrong

When a convention or a section of the Merchant Shipping Act is broken or contravened, the owner, managing agent, Skipper or crew possibly can be prosecuted under that act. There are specific regulations covering collisions, safety equipment, pollution, hours of work etc., and the overarching act covers the whole maritime sector.

Vessels operating under the Small Vessel codes of practice can be prosecuted for breaches within the code or, if they are not coded, prosecuted under the Merchant Shipping Act. The most common parts of the act or legislation to fall foul of are:

Section 100

The part of the Merchant Shipping Act concerning owners and their liability for operating dubiously is Section 100 – Owner liable for unsafe operation of a ship. It applies to any UK ship and any ship within UK waters proceeding to or from a UK port. The requirement is: *It shall be the duty of the owner of a ship to which this section applies to take all reasonable steps to secure that the ship is operated in a safe manner.*

This section also states that the managing agent and the owner can both be held responsible depending on the terms of the contract between them, the offence and the apportion of blame.

It is the responsibility of the owner or managing agent to ensure that the vessel is properly maintained, examined and manned. Owners and managing agents should discuss their respective responsibilities for safety before the vessel goes to sea and state it clearly in the Safety Management System. The maximum penalties under Section 100 are fines of up to £50,000 and up to two years behind bars.

CODE BOAT OPERATES OUTSIDE CERTIFICATION LIMITS

Offence: Breach of Section 100 of the Merchant Shipping Act 1995

Details: The owner Skipper of the MV Invincible took a party of amateur radio enthusiasts from Stromness to Rockall, a distance of more than 200 miles out into the North Atlantic Ocean, despite having been told by the Maritime and Coastguard Agency (MCA) that his boat was not suitable for the voyage.

The group booked the Invincible after finding a web site which advertised that the Skipper had undertaken a similar voyage in the past.

He accepted that he had failed to take all reasonable steps to secure the safe operation of the vessel in that it sailed beyond the distance that it, the Skipper, or the crew were qualified to go and without adequate means of communication.

Penalty: £5,000 fine

(Extract taken from the MCA website – prosecutions and detentions)

Section 58

The Merchant Shipping Act is primarily there to protect those who go to sea by stating that operators of ships equip, man and manage them well. There are also sections that deal with the conduct of seamen. Section 58 – 'Offences by Seamen' covers the outcomes of any action endangering ships, structures or individuals. It applies to the Master or any seaman employed in a UK ship or the Master or seamen employed in any ship within UK waters.

It is enforceable when a person does any act, or is negligent in their duty, which causes or is likely to cause:

- The loss or serious damage to his or another ship, machinery, equipment or structure
- The death or serious injury to a person.

Penalties under Section 58 are fines and up to two years' imprisonment.

TRAWLER FAILS TO KEEP A PROPER LOOKOUT

Date of Offence: *21 May 2008*

Offence: *Failure to keep a proper lookout. Breach of Section 58 of the Merchant Shipping Act 1995, conduct endangering ships, structures or individuals.*

Details: *On 21st May 2008, the trawler ADORATION CN78 was fishing for prawns in upper Loch Fyne. This trawler was seen from the shore to have made contact with buoys marking a fleet of creels, which lay about 200 yards off shore at Inverary. A total of 34 creels were lost.*

Penalty: *Mr ....was fined £400*

(Extract taken from MCA website – prosecutions and detentions)

IRPCS
The COLREGs have similar sober warnings:

Where any of these Regulations is contravened, the owner of the vessel, the Master and any person for the time being responsible for the conduct of the vessel shall each be guilty of an offence, punishable on conviction on indictment by imprisonment for a term not exceeding two years and a fine...

(The Merchant Shipping (Distress Signals and Prevention of Collisions) Regulations 1996)

Offence: *Breach of Collision Regulations – Rule 10 (b)(i)*

Details: *A 36ft motor pleasure vessel was being delivered to a new owner based at a location on the River Crouch in Essex from Brighton. The delivery Skipper for this journey was..... Mr.... is an experienced Skipper who owns his own motor boat and holds appropriate Royal Yachting Association qualifications.*

At approximately 10.40 a.m. the vessel entered the South West shipping lane in the Dover Straits Traffic Separation Scheme (TSS). Mr.... then took the vessel in a north easterly direction against the general flow of traffic. The vessel continued in this lane for approximately 50 minutes travelling about 15 miles before exiting the South West lane and re-entering the Inshore Traffic Zone. During this period the vessel passed relatively close to three large merchant ships that were travelling in a south westerly direction.

The Chairman of the Bench said that there were four aggravating factors in this case:

- *The speed and distance of transgression;*
- *The experience of the Skipper;*
- *It was a commercial voyage;*
- *A significant error in navigation*

Penalty: *Mr.... was fined £6,000 plus costs of £2,084.45. In arriving at the fine they took into account his early guilty plea and co-operation with the MCA.*

(Extract taken from MCA website – prosecutions and detentions)

Drugs and Alcohol

Laws concerning the consumption of alcohol and drugs by a professional seaman are similar in a way to the drink-driving laws in the UK as they use similar limits. However, the laws are possibly even more far-reaching as they cover, in effect, when you are on duty and also when you are not on duty but in the event of an emergency you need to take action to protect the safety of passengers.

The consequence is that even when the boat is safely tied up and not going anywhere, if there are passengers on-board, anybody responsible for the safety of the passengers must stay within the prescribed limits.

Vessels with multiple crew may need to draw up a rota so that there are defined safety personnel who must stay within legal limits, even when 'off-duty' but on-board.

In general terms, a person commits an offence if their ability to carry out their duties is impaired because of drink or drugs.

The laws are in three sections and are covered in 'The Railway and Transport Safety Act 2003 Pt 4'.

Sections 78 and 79 concern professional seamen and Skippers. Section 80 covers non-professionals. While Sections 78 and 79 have been brought into force, Section 80 has not.

Both non-professionals and professionals can also be prosecuted under the Merchant Shipping Act under Section 58 (Offences by Seamen) and one or two other sections, if sections 78 and 79 of the Railway and Transport Safety Act do not stick.

Penalty on conviction under the Railway and Transport Safety Act is up to two years' imprisonment and/or a fine.

Negligence

Negligence is proved when someone has omitted to do something that a reasonable person should have done or that same prudent person would not do. As a Skipper and/or owner, you have a duty to care for those on-board and if through your actions they sustain injury or damage you are said to be negligent. Negligence comes under the Law of Torts which also encompasses liability, deceit, falsehood and defamation.

Removal of Certification

Vessels, Skippers and crew can lose their certification. Certification is granted by the authority and can be withdrawn if due cause is shown. Vessels have been detained, restricted in their use, seized and taken off the UK register. Skippers and crew have had their personal qualifications, such as RYA Yachtmaster qualifications, suspended and withdrawn.

Annex 1

Guidance on the Composition of a Navigational Watch (STCW Section A-VIII/2/16)

In determining that the composition of the navigational watch is adequate to ensure that a proper look-out can be continuously maintained, the Master should take into account all relevant factors including the following:

- Visibility, state of weather and sea
- Traffic density and other activities occurring in the area in which the ship is navigating
- The attention necessary when navigating in or near traffic-separation schemes or other routeing measures
- The additional workload caused by the nature of the ship's functions, immediate operating requirements and anticipated manoeuvres
- The fitness for duty of any crew members on call who are assigned as members of the watch
- Knowledge of and confidence in the professional competence of the ship's officers and crew
- The experience of each OOW (Officer of Watch), and the familiarity of that OOW with the ship's equipment, procedures and manoeuvring capability
- Activities taking place on-board the ship at any particular time, including radiocommunication activities, and the availability of assistance to be summoned immediately to the bridge when necessary
- The operational status of bridge instrumentation and controls, including alarm systems
- Rudder and propeller control and ship manoeuvring characteristics
- The size of the ship and the field of vision available from the conning position
- The configuration of the bridge, to the extent such configuration might inhibit a member of the watch from detecting by sight or hearing any external development
- Any other relevant standard, procedure or guidance relating to watchkeeping arrangements and fitness for duty

Annex 2

Guidance on Regulations for UK Pleasure Vessels and Yachts

All vessels must comply with the SOLAS Chapter V and the COLREGs. Specific guidance on the application of other conventions and regulations are given in the links below.

Pleasure Vessels

The MCA guidance is given in the MCA document 'Information on the Regulations Applicable to Pleasure Vessels':

http://www.direct.gov.uk/prod_consum_dg/groups/dg_digitalassets/@dg/@en/documents/digitalasset/dg_185782.pdf

Small Commercial Vessels (<24m)

The guidance for these vessels is contained in the small commercial vessel codes of practice:

http://www.businesslink.gov.uk/bdotg/action/detail?itemId=1087198454&type=RESOURCES

or the MCA Code Information Pack:

http://www.dft.gov.uk/mca/mcga07-home/shipsandcargoes/mcga-shiptype/mcga-pleasurecraftandsmallships/mcga-dqs-cvs-newsletter.htm

Large Yachts used for Sport or Pleasure

Yachts >24m carrying up to 12 passengers are covered by the Large Yacht Code:

http://www.dft.gov.uk/mca/mcga07-home/shipsandcargoes/ensign/dops_-_east_ensign_ly2-2.htm

Annex 3

Skippered Charter – Safety Briefing

Before the commencement of any voyage the Skipper should ensure that all persons on-board are briefed, as a minimum, on the stowage and use of personal safety equipment such as lifejackets, thermal protective aids and lifebuoys, and the procedures to be followed in cases of emergency.

In addition to this, the Skipper should brief at least one other person who will be sailing on the voyage regarding the following:

- Location of liferafts and the method of launching
- Procedures for the recovery of a person from the sea
- Location and use of pyrotechnics
- Procedures and operation of radios carried on-board
- Location of navigation and other light switches
- Location and use of fire-fighting equipment
- Method of starting, stopping, and controlling the main engine
- Method of navigating to a suitable port of refuge
- Location of Stability Guidance Booklet, and Stability Information Booklet, if applicable

Safety cards will be considered an acceptable way of providing the above information.

Annex 4

Handover Procedures for Owners/Managing Agents who Bareboat Charter

Familiarisation at Handover

The owner/managing agent or appointed representative with intimate knowledge of the vessel should be present at the handover of the vessel to the chartering Skipper and crew in order to complete, as a minimum, the following familiarisation process:

- A demonstration of the stowage of all gear and the method of use of all lifesaving and fire-fighting appliances on-board the vessel should be given
- The location and method of operation of all sea cocks and bilge pumps should be explained
- A demonstration to ensure familiarisation with all mechanical, electrical and electronic equipment should be carried out
- Details of routine maintenance required for any equipment should be declared
- Checks to be carried out on the engine prior to starting, while running and after stopping to be demonstrated
- The method of setting, sheeting and reefing each sail should be shown

Documentation

The owner/managing agent or appointed representative should ensure that the vessel's file is shown to the chartering Skipper. The vessel's file should contain at least the following:

- Registration papers
- Copies of the insurance policy
- Other necessary certificates
- Details of permitted operating area
- Instruction manuals
- Electrical wiring and piping/plumbing diagrams
- Inventory of the vessel's equipment
- Plan(s) showing the stowage position of all the movable equipment necessary for the safe operation of the vessel
- A list of names and telephone numbers (both in and out of office hours) of persons who may be contacted if the chartering Skipper or the vessel is in need of assistance

The owner/managing agent or appointed representative should ensure that the Stability Guidance Booklet and Stability Information Booklet (if applicable) are shown to the chartering Skipper.

The Skipper chartering the vessel should sign an acceptance note after the handover procedure with regard to the inventory, condition of items demonstrated and the amounts of fuel and other consumable items on-board which may be chargeable.

Procedure on Return of the Vessel to the Owner/Managing Agent
At the end of the charter the owner/managing agent or appointed representative, together with the chartering Skipper, should observe the following procedure:

- The chartering Skipper should advise the owner/managing agent of any lost or damaged equipment
- The chartering Skipper should advise the owner/managing agent of any defects or damage to the vessel
- The owner/managing agent should be present to review any matter deemed important
- The above details should be noted on an appropriate form which is to be signed by the owner/managing agent or appointed representative and the chartering Skipper

Annex 5

MAIB Reporting Requirements and Definitions

Subject to 2 below,

1. Accidents involving or occurring on-board –

   (a) any United Kingdom ship, must be reported to the MAIB under the Regulations.

2. Accidents involving or occurring on-board –

   (a) a pleasure vessel
   (b) a recreational craft hired on a bareboat basis
   (c) any other craft or boat, other than one carrying passengers, which is in commercial use in a harbour or on an inland waterway and is less than 8m in length

   do not need to be reported to the MAIB, unless the accident involves

   (i) explosion
   (ii) fire
   (iii) death
   (iv) major injury
   (v) capsize of a power-driven craft or boat, or
   (vi) pollution causing significant harm to the environment

3. Accidents involving or occurring on-board non-UK ships –

   (a) within the jurisdiction of a harbour master or Queen's harbour master

   (b) carrying passengers to or from a port in the United Kingdom

   must be reported to the MAIB under the Regulations.

4. Accidents involving shore-based workers while a ship is in port or in a shipyard within the United Kingdom should be reported by the person's employer to the Health and Safety Executive. No report to the MAIB is required.

5. Accidents involving divers while diving are not covered by the Regulations. Any such incident should be reported to the British Sub Aqua Club. No report to the MAIB is required.

Accidents and Major & Serious Injuries

1. **Accident** means any occurrence on-board a ship or involving a ship whereby –

    (a) there is loss of life or major injury to any person on-board, or any person is lost or falls overboard from, the ship or one of its ship's boats;

    (b) a ship –

    - **(i)** causes any loss of life, major injury or material damage;
    - **(ii)** is lost or presumed to be lost;
    - **(iii)** is abandoned;
    - **(iv)** is materially damaged by fire, explosion, weather or other cause;
    - **(v)** grounds;
    - **(vi)** is in collision;
    - **(vii)** is disabled; or
    - **(viii)** causes significant harm to the environment.

    (c) any of the following occur –

    - **(i)** a collapse or bursting of any pressure vessel, pipeline or valve;
    - **(ii)** a collapse or failure of any lifting equipment, access equipment, hatch-cover, staging or boatswain's chair or any associated load-bearing parts;
    - **(iii)** a collapse of cargo, unintended movement of cargo or ballast sufficient to cause a list, or loss of cargo overboard;
    - **(iv)** a snagging of fishing gear which results in the vessel heeling to a dangerous angle;
    - **(v)** a contact by a person with loose asbestos fibre except when full protective clothing is worn; or
    - **(vi)** an escape of any harmful substance or agent, if the occurrence, taking into account its circumstances, might have been liable to cause serious injury or to cause damage to the health of any person.

    The terms "disabled" and "grounds" are separately defined.

2. **Major injury** means –

(a) any fracture, other than to a finger, thumb or toe;

(b) any loss of a limb or part of a limb;

(c) dislocation of the shoulder, hip, knee or spine;

(d) loss of sight, whether temporary or permanent;

(e) penetrating injury to the eye; or

(f) any other injury –

(i) leading to hypothermia or to unconsciousness, or

(ii) requiring resuscitation, or

(iii) requiring admittance to a hospital or other medical facility as an in-patient for more than 24 hours.

3. Serious injury means any injury, other than a major injury, to a person employed or carried in a ship which occurs on-board or during access which results in incapacity for more than three consecutive days excluding the day of the accident or as a result of which the person concerned is put ashore and the ship sails without that person, unless the incapacity is known or advised to be of three consecutive days or less, excluding the day of the accident.

Annex 6

Salvage and Towing

Towage is a contract for assisting the voyage of a vessel when nothing more is required than 'accelerating her progress'. There is very little chance of a tug claiming salvage if it is contracted to tow another unless the towing situation seriously deteriorates through conditions.

The International Convention on Salvage, 1989 defines a 'salvage operation' as any act or activity undertaken to assist a vessel or any other property in danger in navigable waters or in any other waters whatsoever. 'Vessel' means any ship or craft, or any structure capable of navigation.

Therefore, a vessel or person coming to your aid to tow, pilot, navigate, advise or stand-by can be termed as a salvageable act. The amount a salvor is paid is determined by the risk that he takes and what life or property he saves. Do not be fooled by appearances; even the British and French navies have claimed salvage against yachts.

Try to agree a towage figure first. If you can't or don't, state 'No Cure, No Pay' and agree on Lloyd's open or standard form where the salvage fee can be fixed by arbitration after the event.

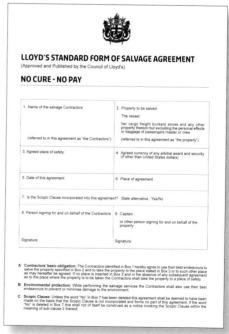

LLOYD'S STANDARD FORM OF SALVAGE AGREEMENT
(Approved and Published by the Council of Lloyd's)

NO CURE - NO PAY

1. Name of the salvage Contractors:	2. Property to be salved:
	The vessel:
	her cargo freight bunkers stores and any other property thereon but excluding the personal effects or baggage of passengers master or crew
(referred to in this agreement as 'the Contractors')	(referred to in this agreement as 'the property')
3. Agreed place of safety:	4. Agreed currency of any arbitral award and security (if other than United States dollars)
5. Date of this agreement	6. Place of agreement
7. Is the Scopic Clause incorporated into this agreement? State alternative : Yes/No	
8. Person signing for and on behalf of the Contractors	9. Captain
	or other person signing for and on behalf of the property
Signature:	Signature:

A **Contractors' basic obligation:** The Contractors identified in Box 1 hereby agree to use their best endeavours to salve the property specified in Box 2 and to take the property to the place stated in Box 3 or to such other place as may hereafter be agreed. If no place is inserted in Box 3 and in the absence of any subsequent agreement as to the place where the property is to be taken the Contractors shall take the property to a place of safety.

B **Environmental protection:** While performing the salvage services the Contractors shall also use their best endeavours to prevent or minimise damage to the environment.

C **Scopic Clause:** Unless the word 'No' in Box 7 has been deleted this agreement shall be deemed to have been made on the basis that the Scopic Clause is not incorporated and forms no part of this agreement. If the word 'No' is deleted in Box 7 this shall not of itself be construed as a notice invoking the Scopic Clause within the meaning of sub-clause 2 thereof.

If you are in a stressful situation where communication is difficult, try to show that you still have some control of the situation by using your own line, gathering and recording forecasts and keeping an accurate log. This can be used in your defence if the case goes to court or arbitration. Any verbal agreement should be witnessed by the crew and entered in the log.

If no agreement has been made, once ashore, again try to settle a fee for towage and get a receipt.

When towing a vessel, the tug and tow are legally classed as one vessel because they are joined. Whether or not a towage contract is in place changes who is responsible; if the tug is not carrying proper lights and there is a collision, the tow could be held responsible if no contract is in place, whereas if there was a contract, the responsibility would lie with the tug as the service provider.

Standard Forms of Salvage are available from the RYA and Lloyd's of London.

Annex 7

Safety Management System Structure

The International Safety Management (ISM) Code has a structure for the development of a Safety Management System (SMS). The structure is given in The International Safety Management Code IMO Assembly Resolution A.741(18) – 1993.

1. **Definitions** – This section should cover the functional objectives of the SMS and how and to whom it will be applied.

2. **Safety And Environmental Protection Policy** – Policy documents stating how safety and environmental objectives will be achieved and implemented.

3. **Company Responsibilities And Authority** – Outlining the company's responsibilities and detailing who is responsible for what.

4. **Designated Person(s)** – The link between high-level management and the safe operation of each ship.

5. **Master's Responsibility And Authority** – Detailing the Master's responsibility for the crew, passengers and boat whilst in charge.

6. **Resources And Personnel** – Responsibilities of all for ensuring appropriate training, certification, experience of crew, knowledge of systems.

7. **Development Of Plans For Shipboard Operations** – Operational procedures for the safe running of the boat and how acts are performed.

8. **Emergency Preparedness** – Responsibility for training and drills in emergency situations.

9. **Reports And Analysis Of Non-Conformities, Accidents And Hazardous Occurrences** – Recording and reporting procedures.

10. **Maintenance Of The Ship And Equipment**

11. **Documentation** – Establishing and maintaining procedures to control all documents and data which are relevant to the SMS.

12. **Company Verification, Review And Evaluation** – Ensuring that the whole company, crew, staff and Skippers understand the SMS. Establishing times for review and audit.

13. **Certification, Verification And Control** – SMS certification and verification.

INDEX